BUILDING BLOCKS OF THE HUMAN BODY

THE DIGESTIVE AND URINARY SYSTEMS

Written by Joseph Midthun

Illustrated by Samuel Hiti

a Scott Fetzer company
Chicago

World Book, Inc.
180 North LaSalle Street
Suite 900
Chicago, Illinois 60601
USA

For information about other World Book publications, visit our website at **www.worldbook.com** or call **1-800-WORLDBK (967-5325).**
For information about sales to schools and libraries, call 1-800-975-3250 (United States), or 1-800-837-5365 (Canada).

Library of Congress Cataloging-in-Publication Data for this volume has been applied for.

Building Blocks of the Human Body
ISBN: 978-0-7166-4571-9 (set, hc.)

The Digestive and Urinary Systems
ISBN: 978-0-7166-4575-7 (hc.)

Also available as:
ISBN: 978-0-7166-4583-2 (e-book)

1st printing March 2022

Acknowledgments:
Created by Samuel Hiti and Joseph Midthun
Art by Samuel Hiti
Additional art by David Shephard/The Bright Agency
Additional spot art by Shutterstock
Text by Joseph Midthun

TABLE OF CONTENTS

There is a glossary on page 39. Terms defined in the glossary are in type **that looks like this** on their first appearance.

WHY EAT?

Do you know why you have to eat?

Or drink water?

Food and water give your body the materials it needs to live and grow!

Your digestive system breaks down food into pieces small enough for your cells to use.

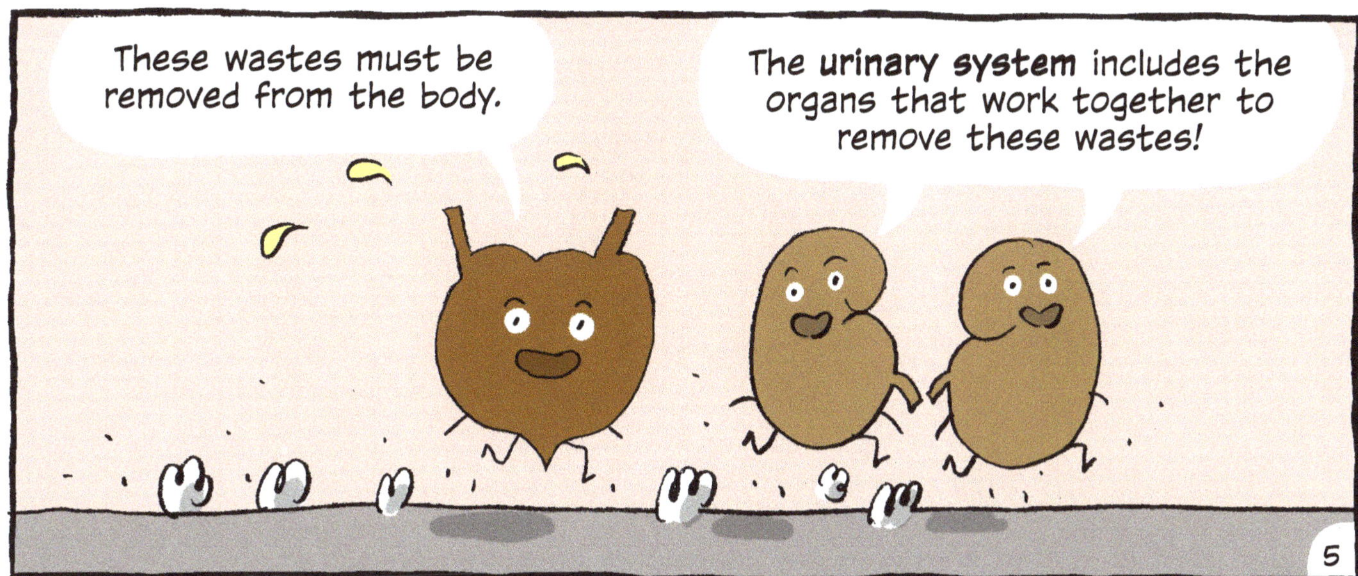

Food contains many different chemicals.
But only a few dozen of these chemicals are needed to keep you healthy.
These few dozen are called **nutrients**.
Let's look at some of the main kinds of nutrients!

Proteins are one of the most important building blocks of the body.
They make up a large part of each cell in the body.
Your muscles and skin are mostly proteins.

Fats and carbohydrates provide energy.
Your body needs energy to run, walk, sit, sleep, and even think and digest.

Your body gets this energy by breaking down fats and carbohydrates, along with proteins.
Vitamins and minerals are needed for growing and repairing parts of the body.
They also take part in many chemical processes in the body. Each vitamin and mineral does a different job.

About two-thirds of your body is made up of water, a vital substance that helps keep your body working properly.
Your digestive system makes sure all of these nutrients get absorbed by the body so that they can be used!

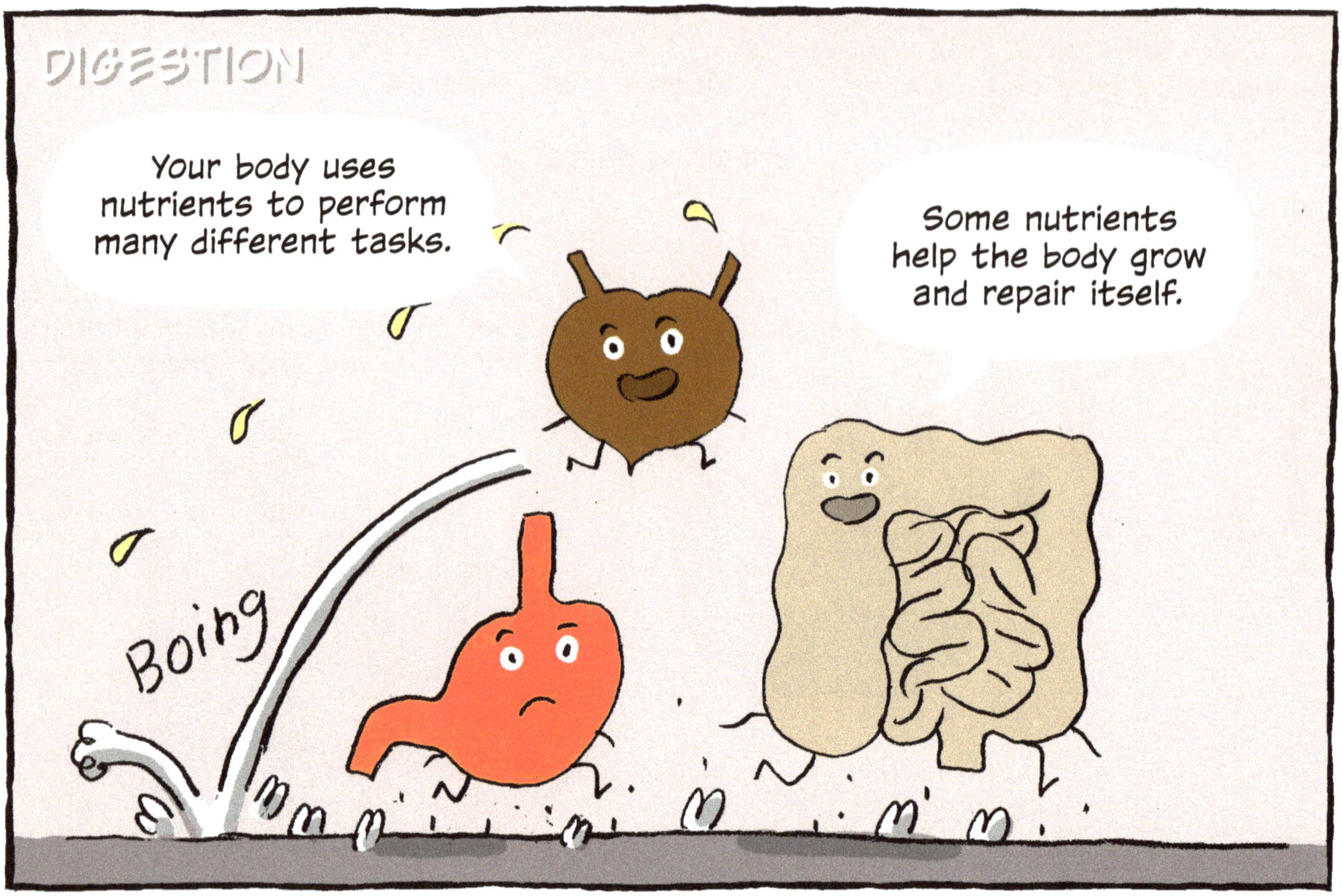

Your body uses nutrients to perform many different tasks.

Some nutrients help the body grow and repair itself.

Boing

Others help your brain and other parts of the body to work!

Still others provide the energy needed for your body to perform all of its functions.

The process of breaking down food into nutrients is called **digestion.**
The body can only absorb nutrients when they are broken down into tiny pieces called **molecules.**

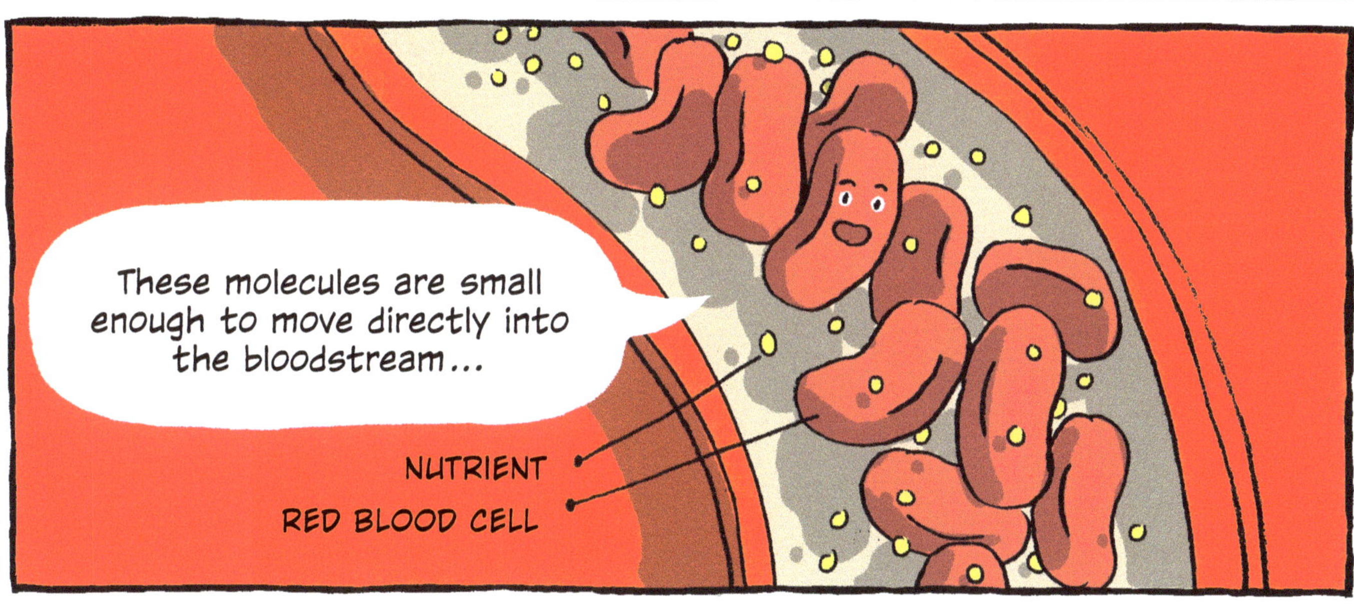
These molecules are small enough to move directly into the bloodstream...
NUTRIENT
RED BLOOD CELL

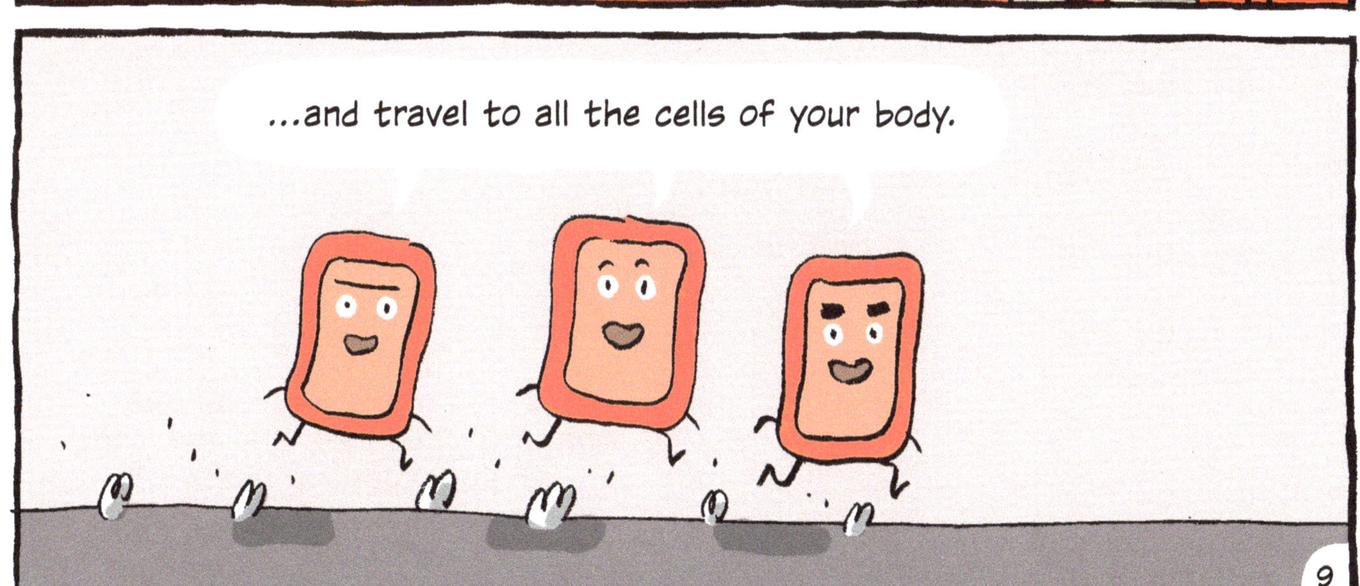
...and travel to all the cells of your body.

PARTS OF THE DIGESTIVE SYSTEM

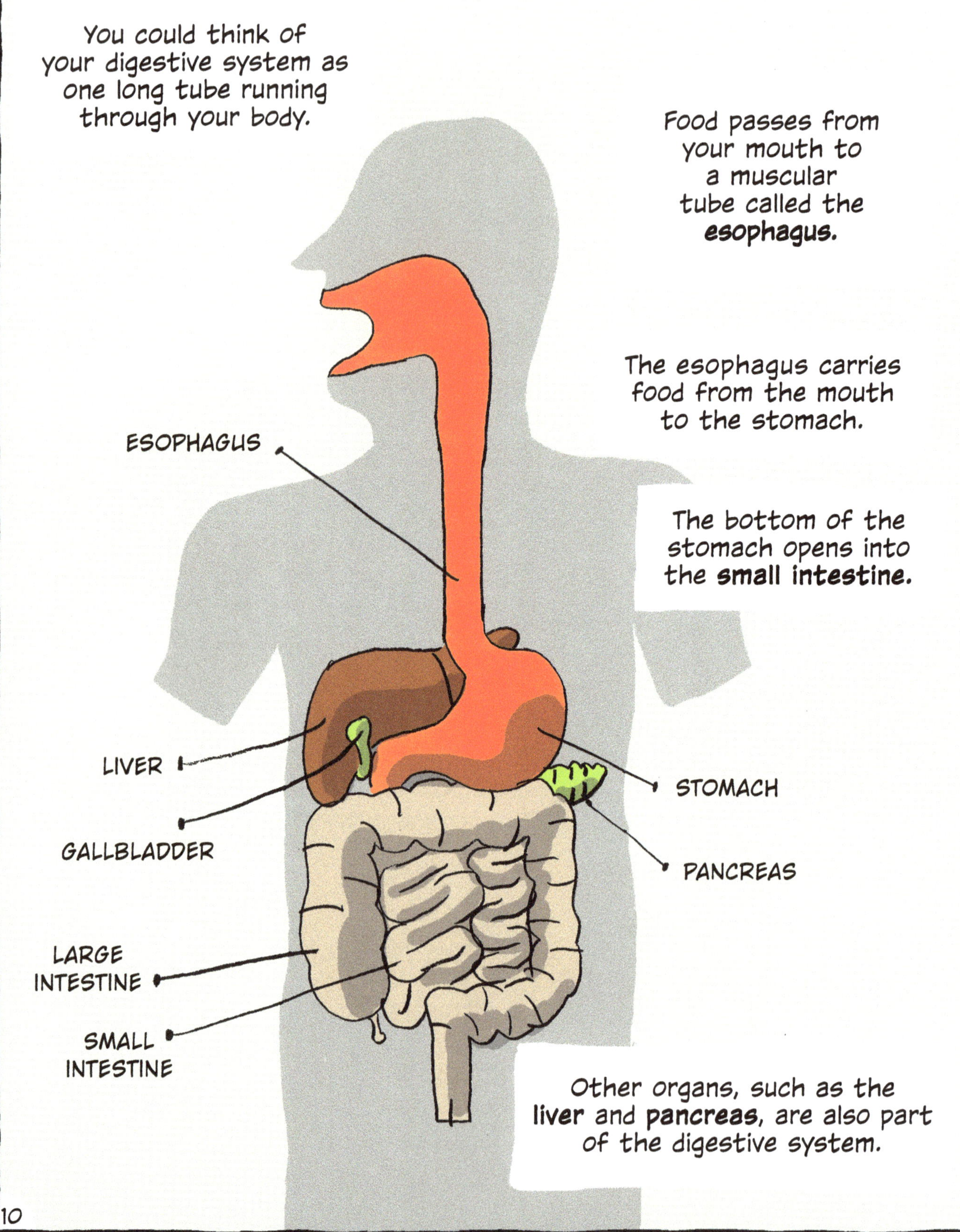

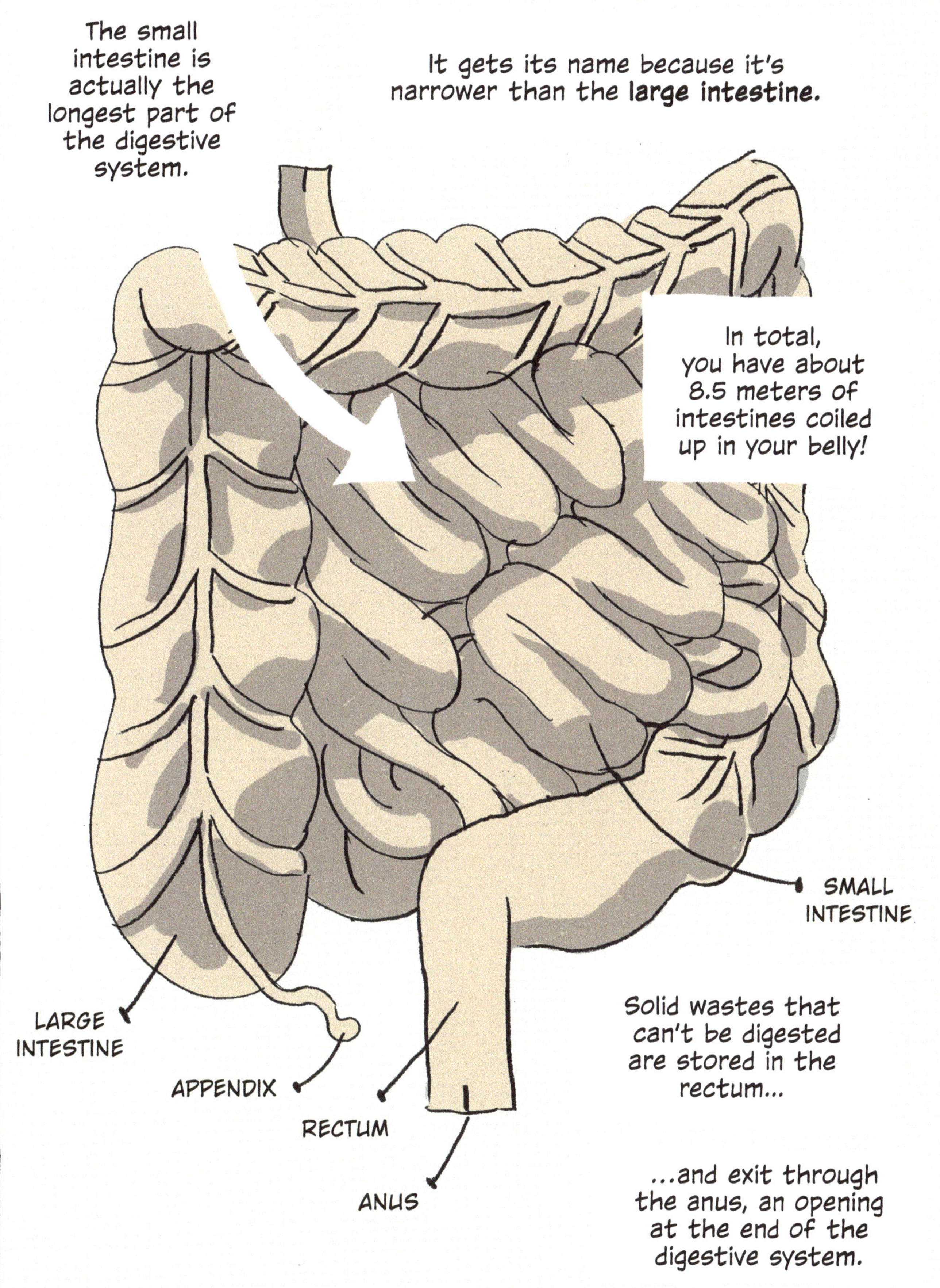
The small intestine is actually the longest part of the digestive system.
It gets its name because it's narrower than the **large intestine.**
In total, you have about 8.5 meters of intestines coiled up in your belly!
SMALL INTESTINE
LARGE INTESTINE
APPENDIX
RECTUM
ANUS
Solid wastes that can't be digested are stored in the rectum...
...and exit through the anus, an opening at the end of the digestive system.

THE MOUTH

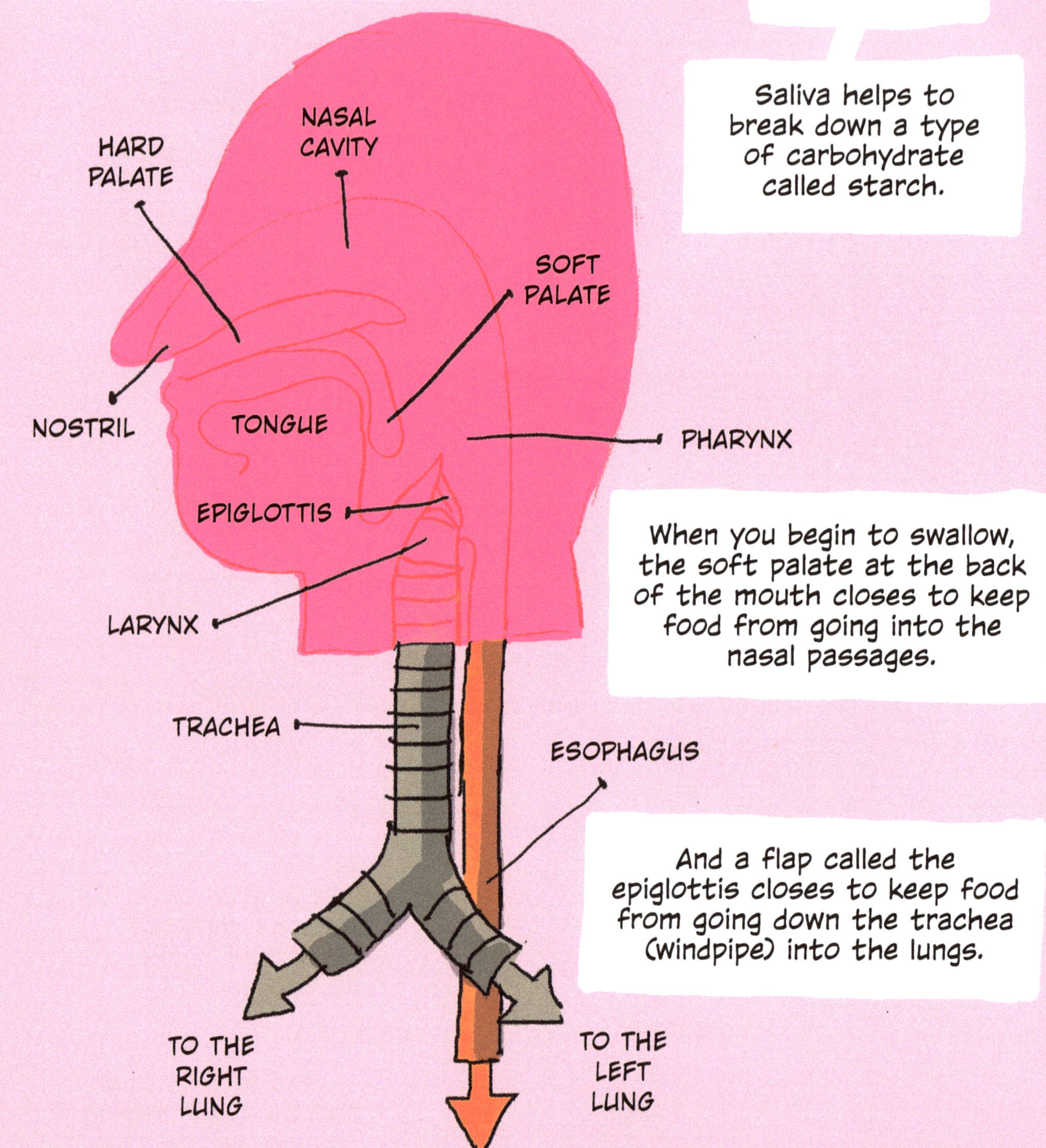

Digestion begins when you take your first bite of food.
When you chew, your teeth break food into smaller and smaller pieces.
Your mouth also produces a liquid called saliva.
Saliva helps to break down a type of carbohydrate called starch.
NASAL CAVITY
HARD PALATE
SOFT PALATE
NOSTRIL
TONGUE
PHARYNX
EPIGLOTTIS
When you begin to swallow, the soft palate at the back of the mouth closes to keep food from going into the nasal passages.
LARYNX
TRACHEA
ESOPHAGUS
And a flap called the epiglottis closes to keep food from going down the trachea (windpipe) into the lungs.
TO THE RIGHT LUNG
TO THE LEFT LUNG
TO THE STOMACH

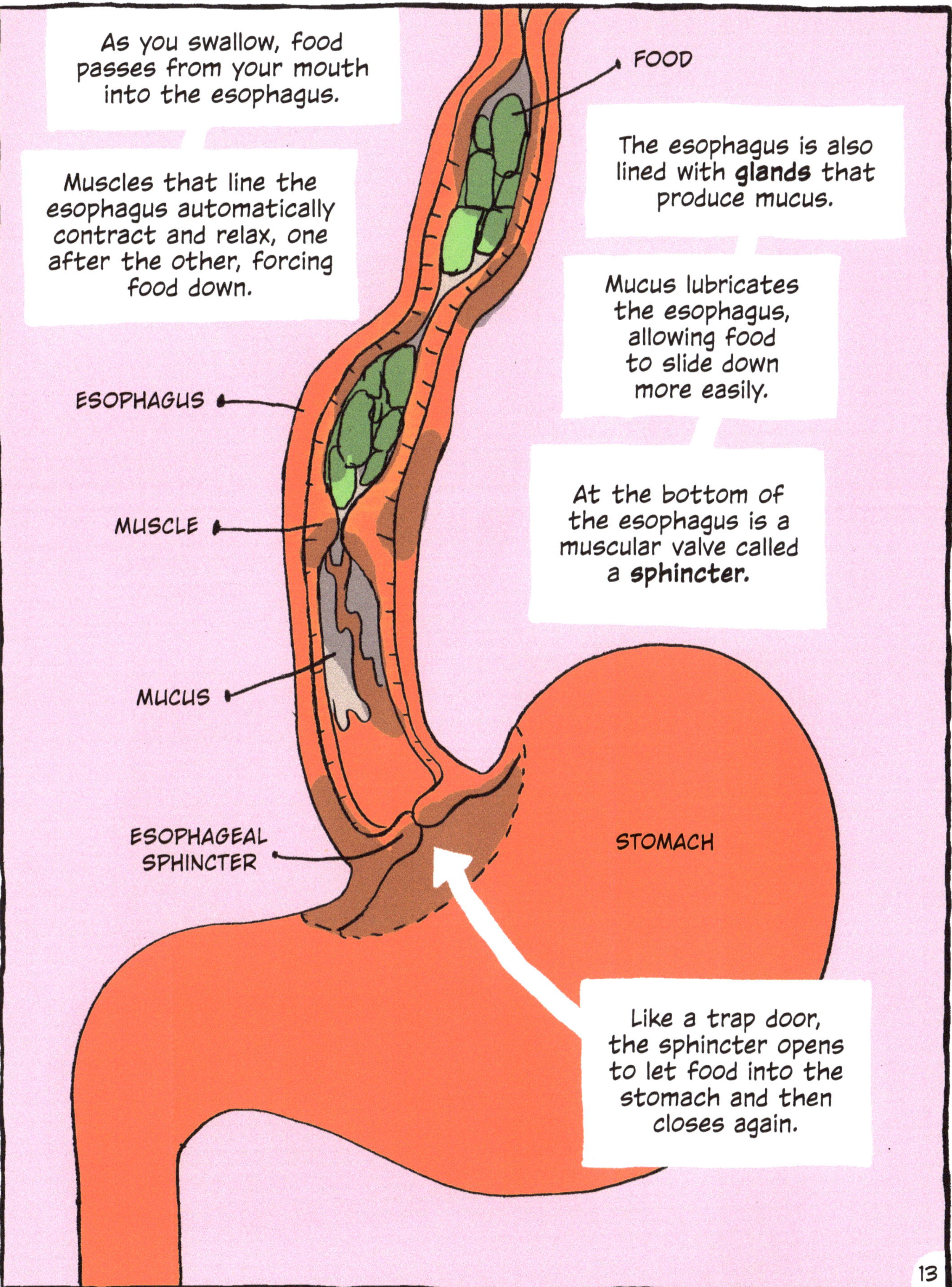
As you swallow, food passes from your mouth into the esophagus.
Muscles that line the esophagus automatically contract and relax, one after the other, forcing food down.
FOOD
The esophagus is also lined with **glands** that produce mucus.
Mucus lubricates the esophagus, allowing food to slide down more easily.
ESOPHAGUS
MUSCLE
At the bottom of the esophagus is a muscular valve called a **sphincter.**
MUCUS
ESOPHAGEAL SPHINCTER
STOMACH
Like a trap door, the sphincter opens to let food into the stomach and then closes again.

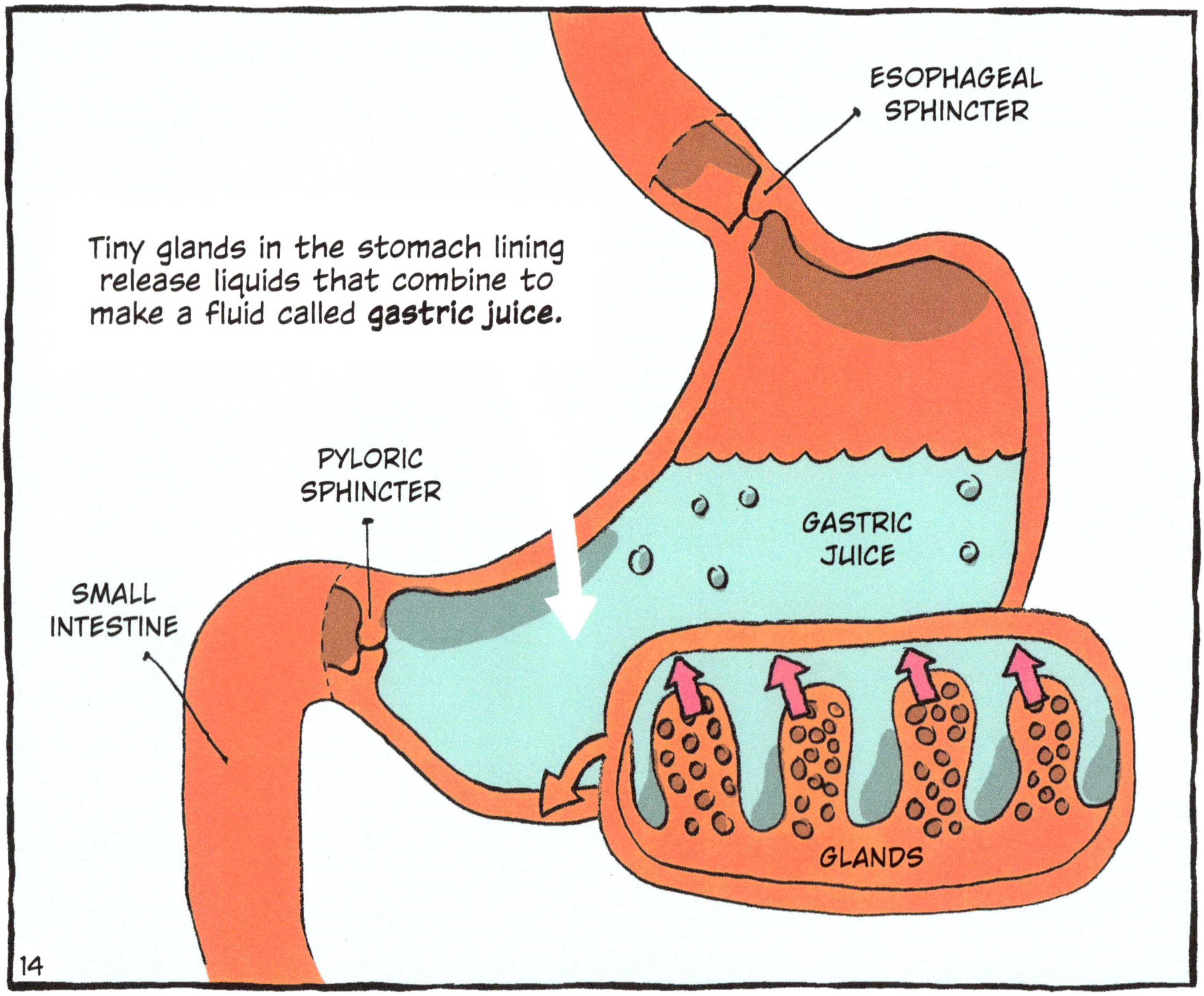

Tiny glands in the stomach lining release liquids that combine to make a fluid called **gastric juice.**

ESOPHAGEAL SPHINCTER

PYLORIC SPHINCTER

GASTRIC JUICE

SMALL INTESTINE

GLANDS

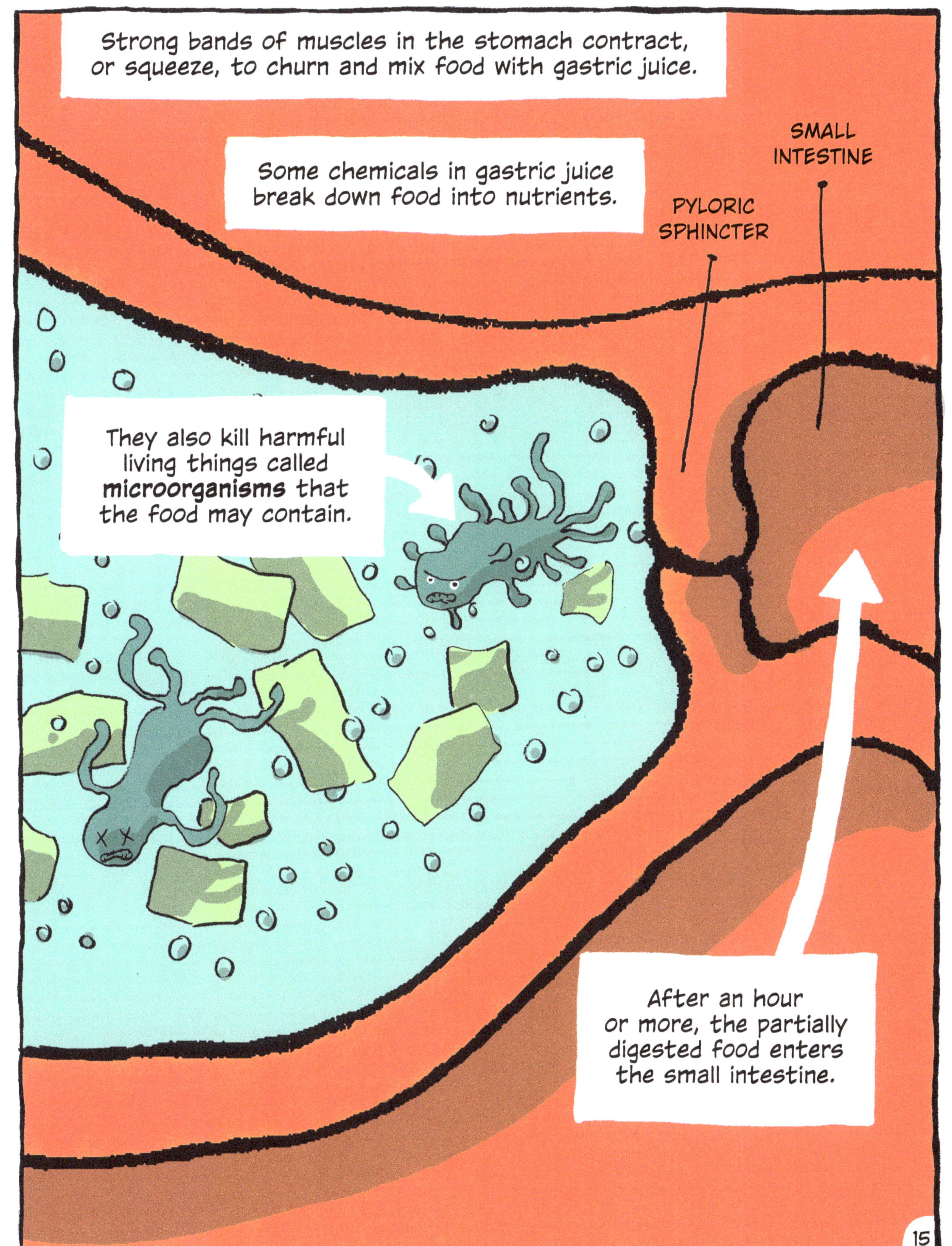
Strong bands of muscles in the stomach contract, or squeeze, to churn and mix food with gastric juice.
Some chemicals in gastric juice break down food into nutrients.
SMALL INTESTINE
PYLORIC SPHINCTER
They also kill harmful living things called **microorganisms** that the food may contain.
After an hour or more, the partially digested food enters the small intestine.

THE SMALL INTESTINE
In the small intestine, partially digested food mixes with juices from several other organs.
These juices break down food even further.

The pancreas sends a juice that helps break down proteins.
The liver sends a greenish-yellow fluid called **bile,** which aids in the digestion of fats.
PANCREAS
LIVER

The **gallbladder** stores excess bile made by the liver and sends it to the small intestine as needed.
GALLBLADDER

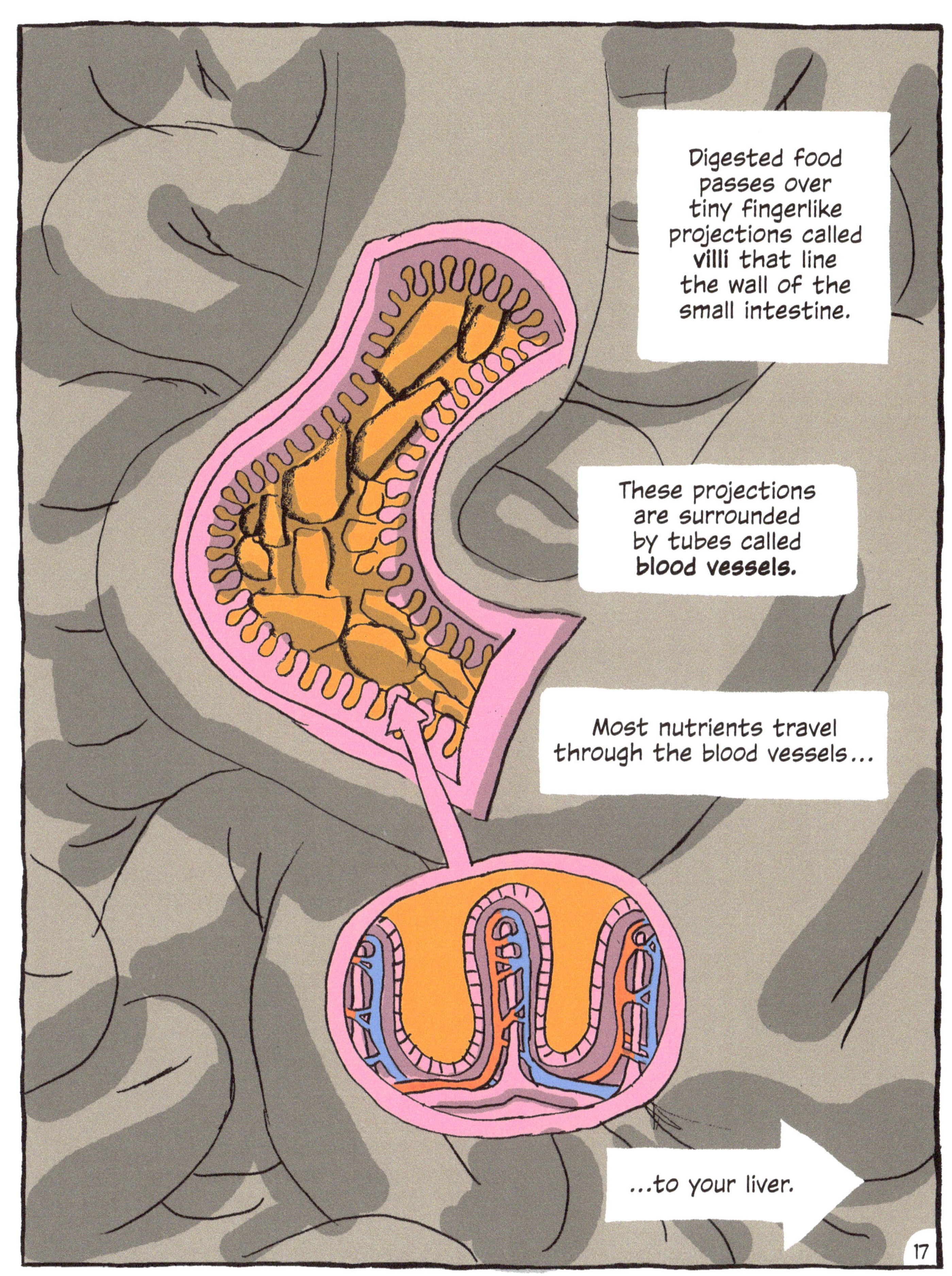
Digested food passes over tiny fingerlike projections called **villi** that line the wall of the small intestine.
These projections are surrounded by tubes called **blood vessels.**
Most nutrients travel through the blood vessels...
...to your liver.

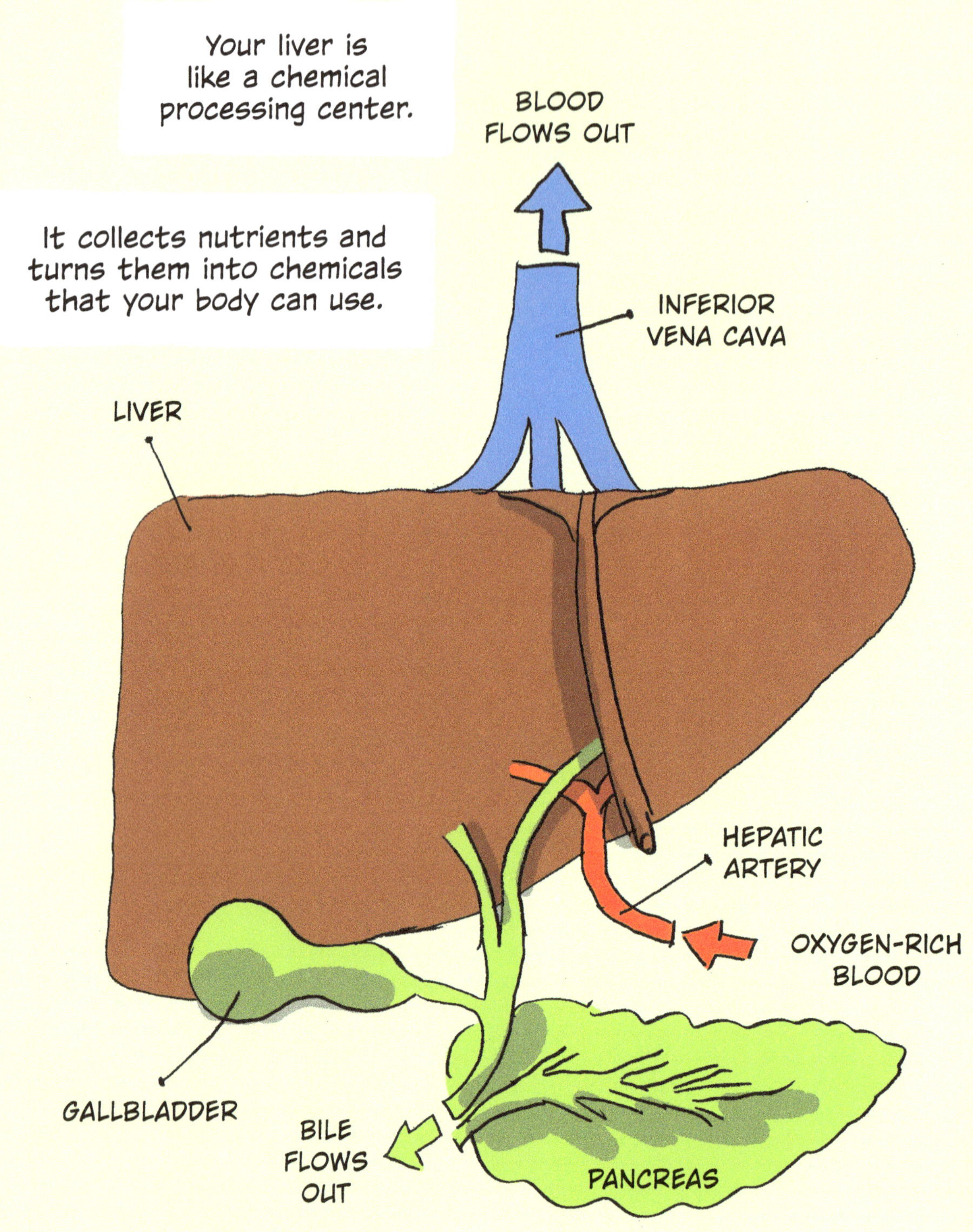
Your liver is like a chemical processing center.
It collects nutrients and turns them into chemicals that your body can use.
BLOOD FLOWS OUT
INFERIOR VENA CAVA
LIVER
HEPATIC ARTERY
OXYGEN-RICH BLOOD
GALLBLADDER
BILE FLOWS OUT
PANCREAS
It releases the chemicals into your bloodstream, where they travel to your cells.

The liver also serves as a storage center.
It saves some of the nutrients from food for later use.

I'm also part of your body's clean-up crew!
mop
mop

squeeze
I find the time to filter poisons and wastes from your blood.

THE LARGE INTESTINE

Your small intestine carries out most of the digestive process.

The remaining undigested material moves to the large intestine...

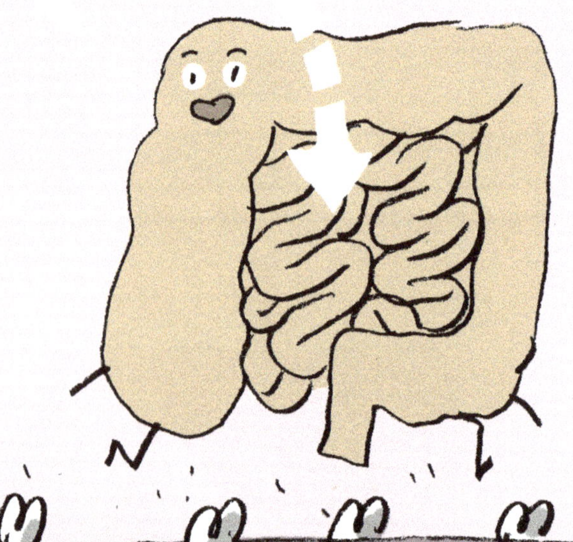

...which absorbs water and salts from this material and eliminates the remaining waste from the body.

This waste is called feces.

About two-thirds of feces is water.

The rest is solid material made up mostly of undigested plant fiber, **bacteria,** and other substances.

Feces are stored in the rectum until you go to the toilet, when they are released through the anus.

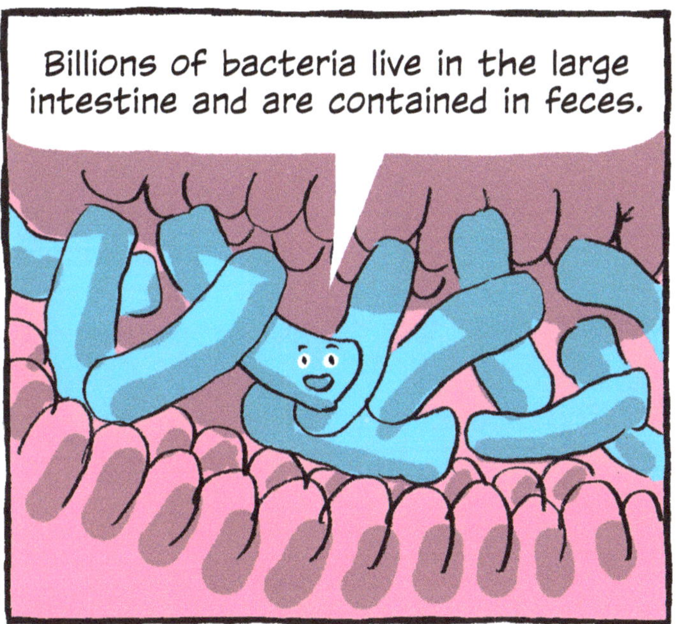
Billions of bacteria live in the large intestine and are contained in feces.

Many are helpful bacteria that help with digestion.

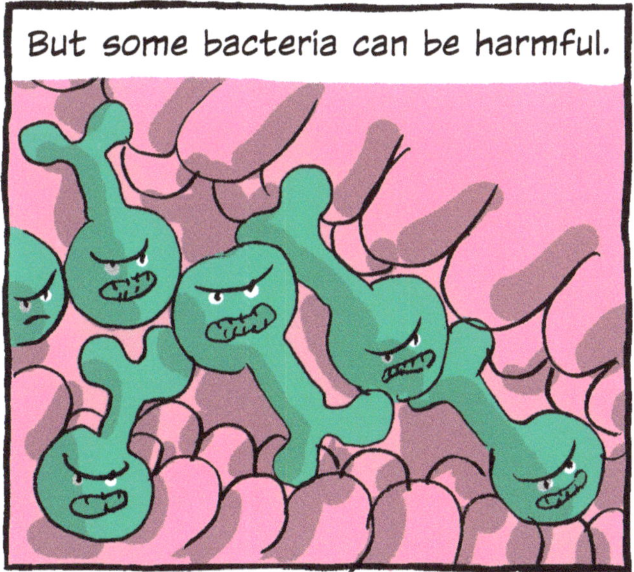
But some bacteria can be harmful.

That's why you should always wash your hands after you go to the bathroom!
SOAP

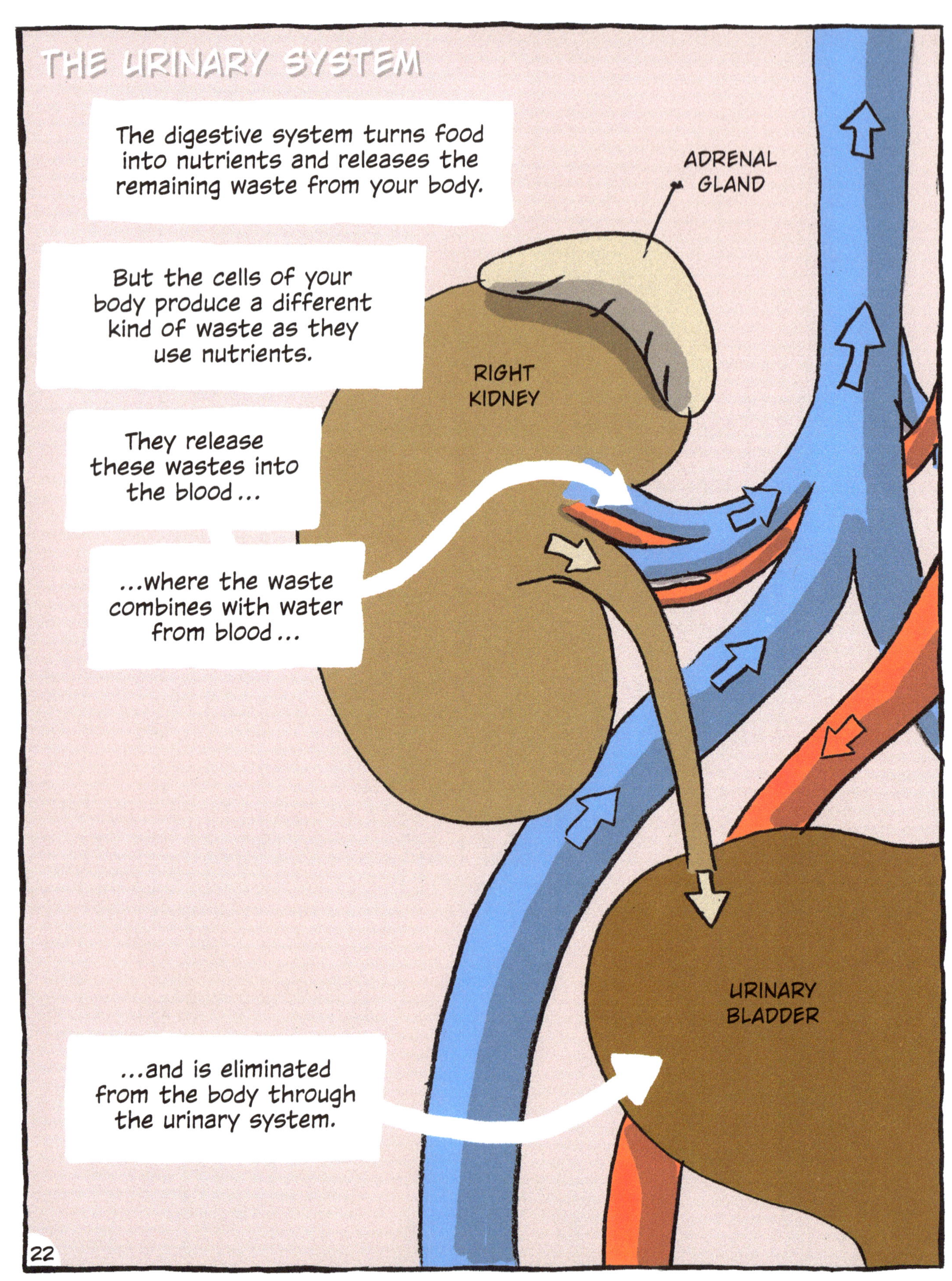
THE URINARY SYSTEM
The digestive system turns food into nutrients and releases the remaining waste from your body.
But the cells of your body produce a different kind of waste as they use nutrients.
They release these wastes into the blood...
...where the waste combines with water from blood...
...and is eliminated from the body through the urinary system.
ADRENAL GLAND
RIGHT KIDNEY
URINARY BLADDER
22

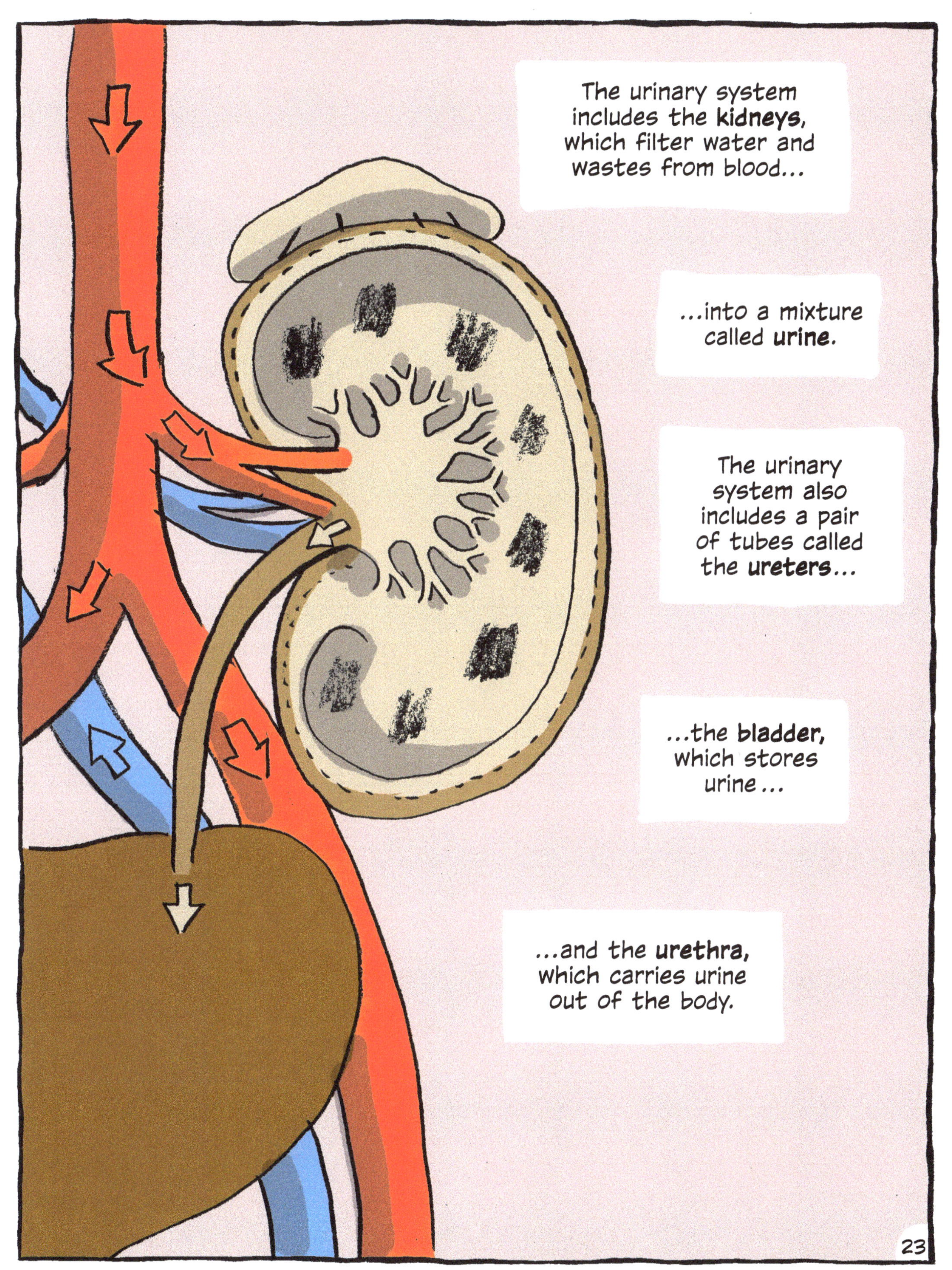
The urinary system includes the **kidneys,** which filter water and wastes from blood...
...into a mixture called **urine.**
The urinary system also includes a pair of tubes called the **ureters**...
...the **bladder,** which stores urine...
...and the **urethra,** which carries urine out of the body.

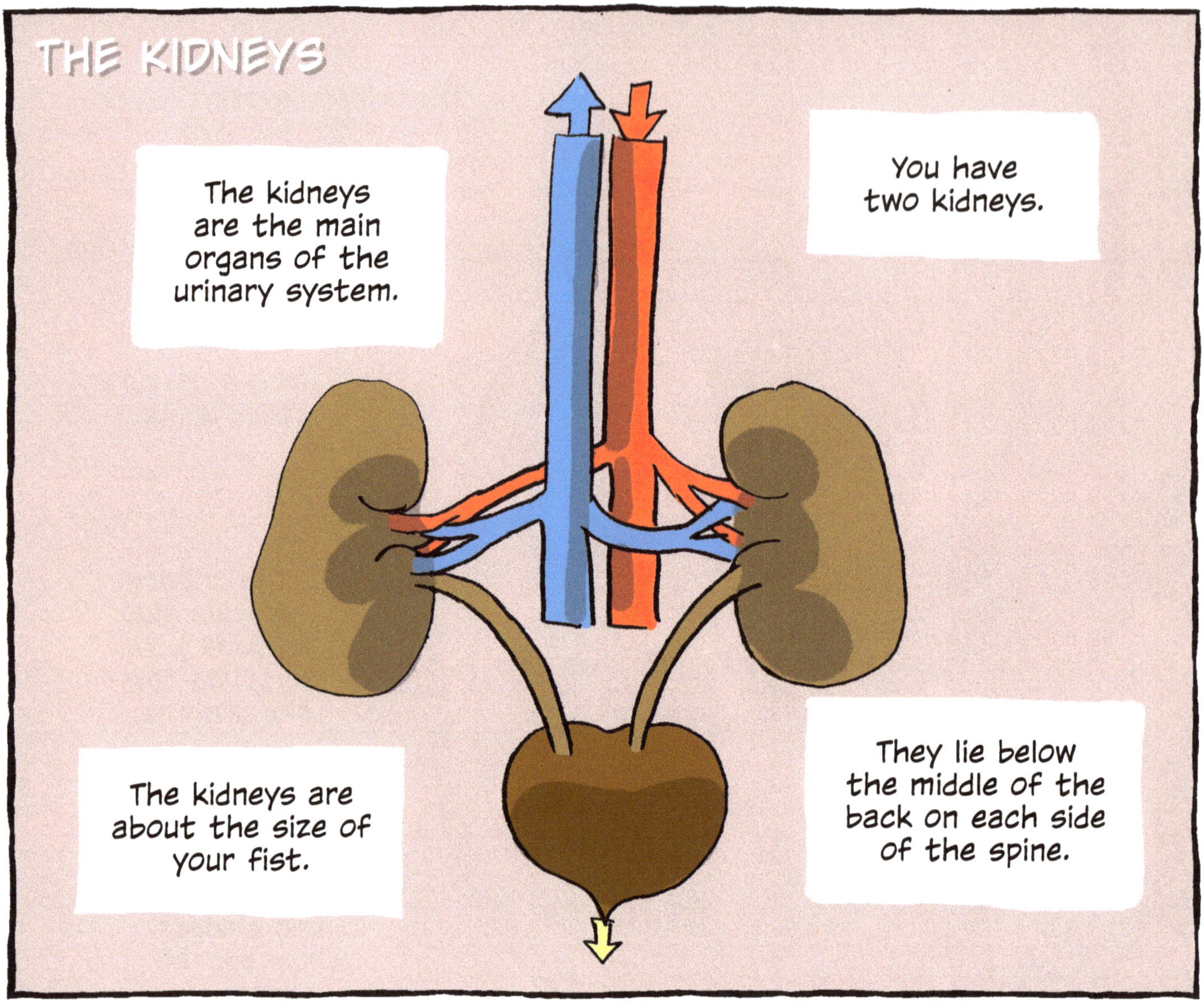

THE KIDNEYS

The kidneys are the main organs of the urinary system.

You have two kidneys.

The kidneys are about the size of your fist.

They lie below the middle of the back on each side of the spine.

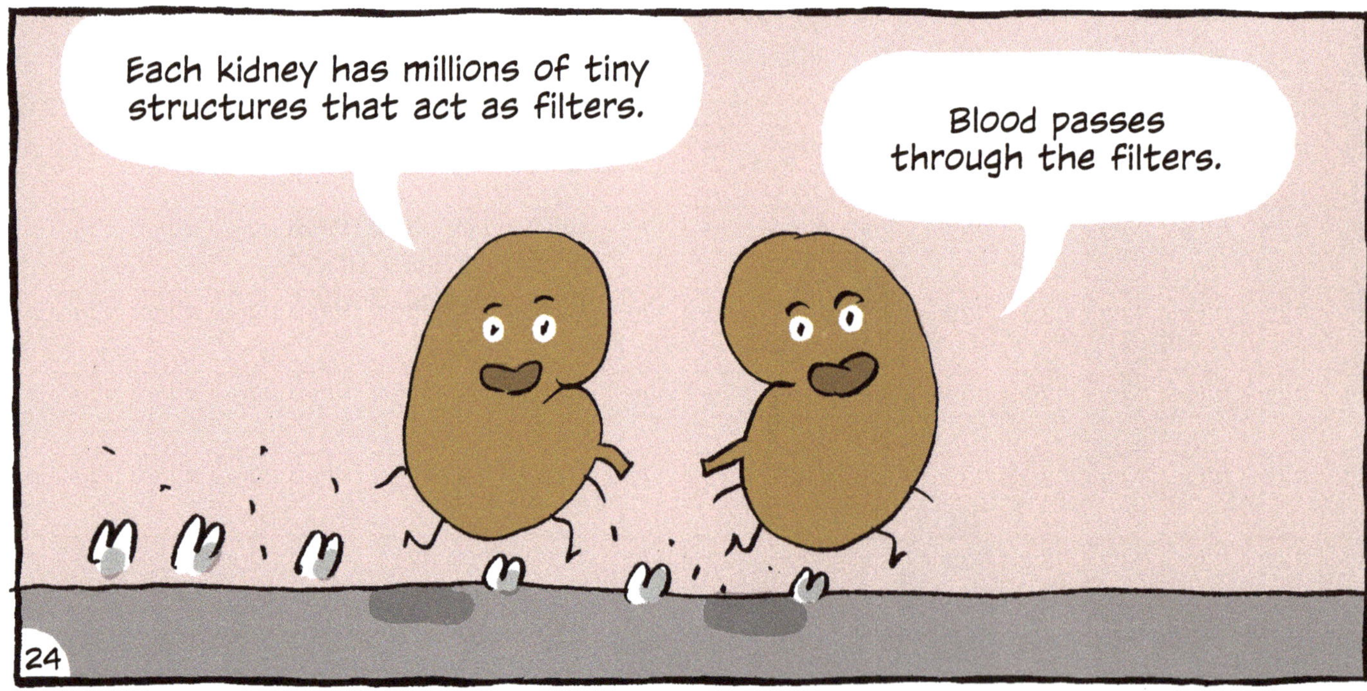

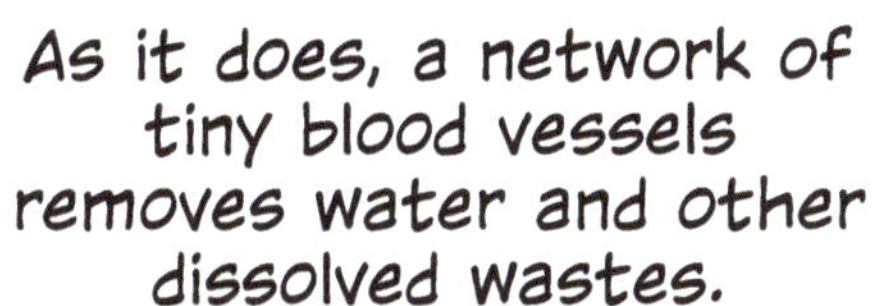
As it does, a network of tiny blood vessels removes water and other dissolved wastes.

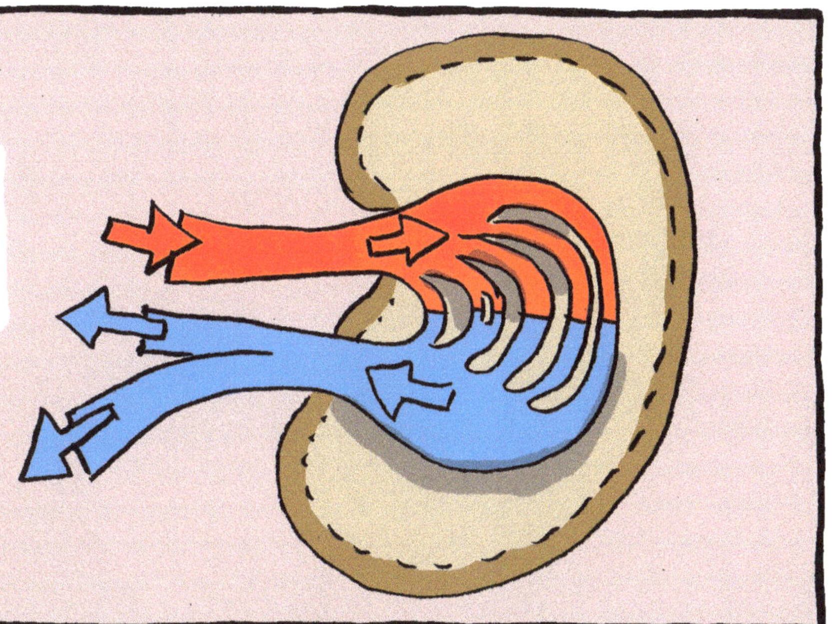

The kidneys return some water and important chemicals to the body.
The remaining material makes up urine.

If the kidneys fail to function, poisons build up in the body, eventually causing death!
OOF!
TUMP
Hey, watch it!

THE URINARY TRACT

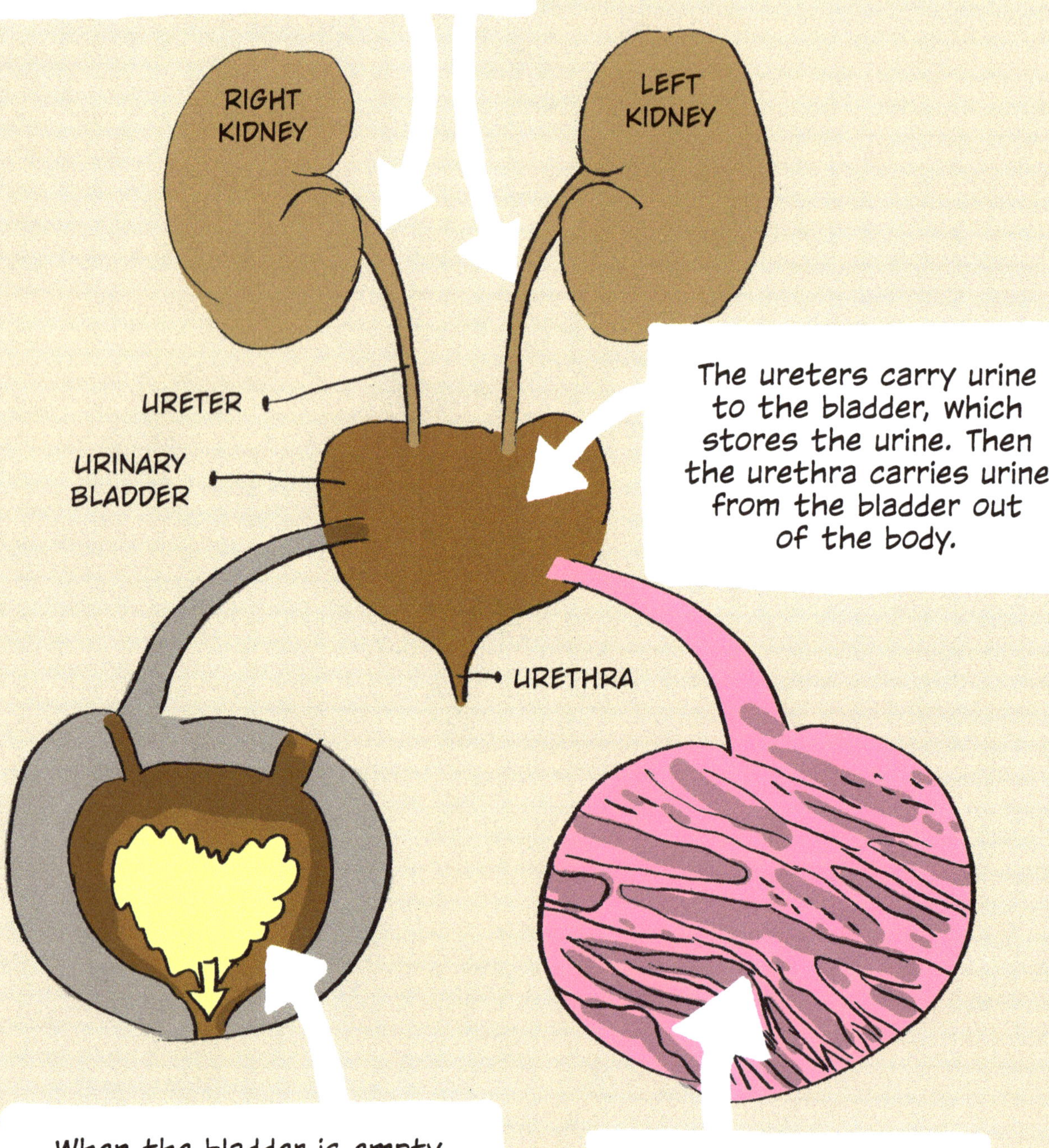

It expands as urine trickles in from the ureters.
The bladder can hold about half a liter of urine.

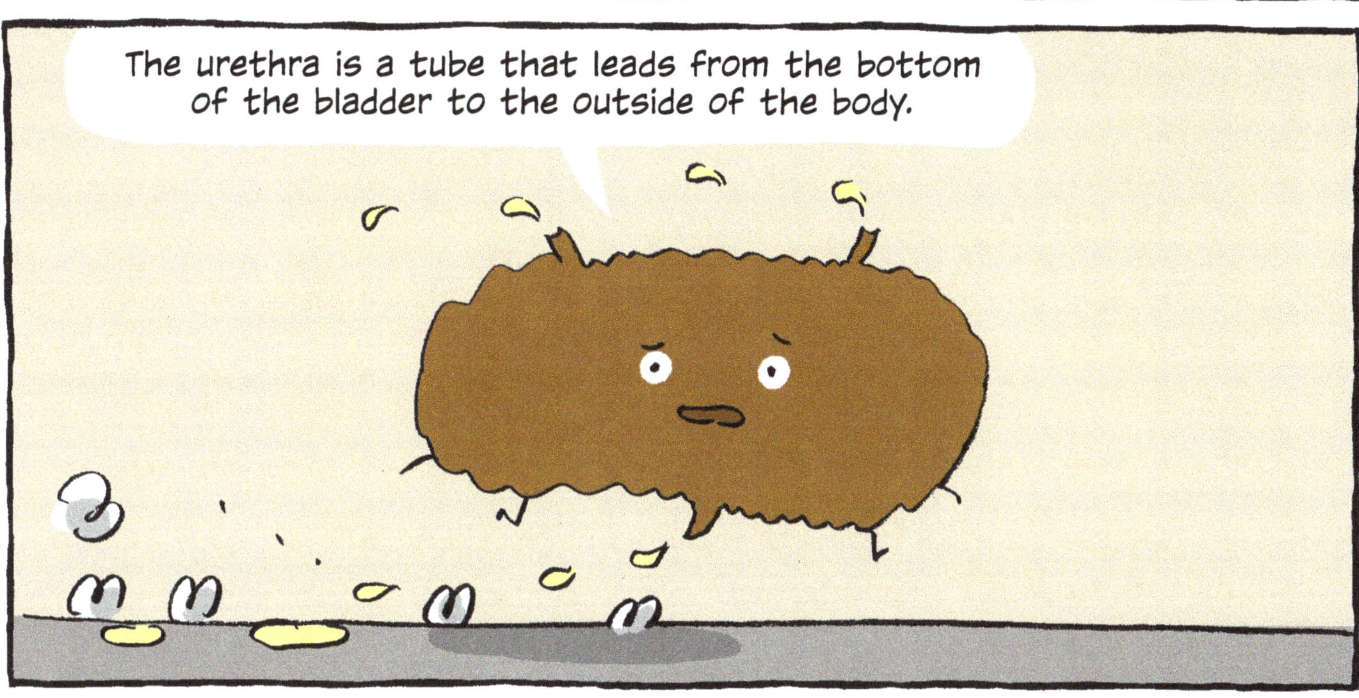
The urethra is a tube that leads from the bottom of the bladder to the outside of the body.

When your bladder is about half full, you begin to feel that you want to go to the bathroom.

HEALTHY DIGESTION
You have to look after your body to keep it working properly.

Drink plenty of water to keep both your digestive and urinary systems running smoothly!
Squirt
water

Roughage, also called dietary fiber, helps keep things moving through your digestive system.

The food you eat affects every cell in your body.

In other words, you really are what you eat!

plop

So choose your food wisely to give yourself a running start in life!

plop

TIMELINE

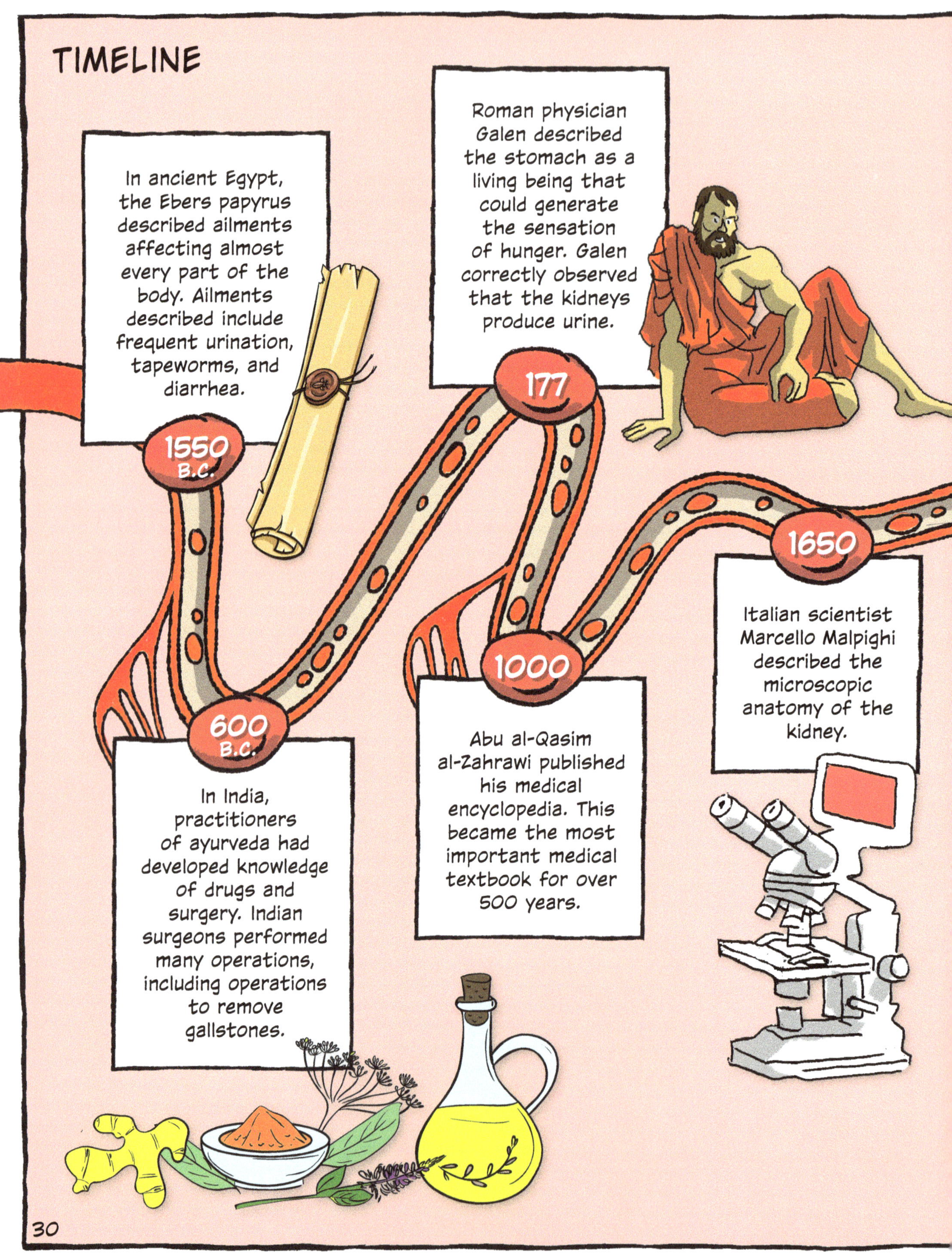

1550 B.C.
In ancient Egypt, the Ebers papyrus described ailments affecting almost every part of the body. Ailments described include frequent urination, tapeworms, and diarrhea.
600 B.C.
In India, practitioners of ayurveda had developed knowledge of drugs and surgery. Indian surgeons performed many operations, including operations to remove gallstones.
177
Roman physician Galen described the stomach as a living being that could generate the sensation of hunger. Galen correctly observed that the kidneys produce urine.
1000
Abu al-Qasim al-Zahrawi published his medical encyclopedia. This became the most important medical textbook for over 500 years.
1650
Italian scientist Marcello Malpighi described the microscopic anatomy of the kidney.

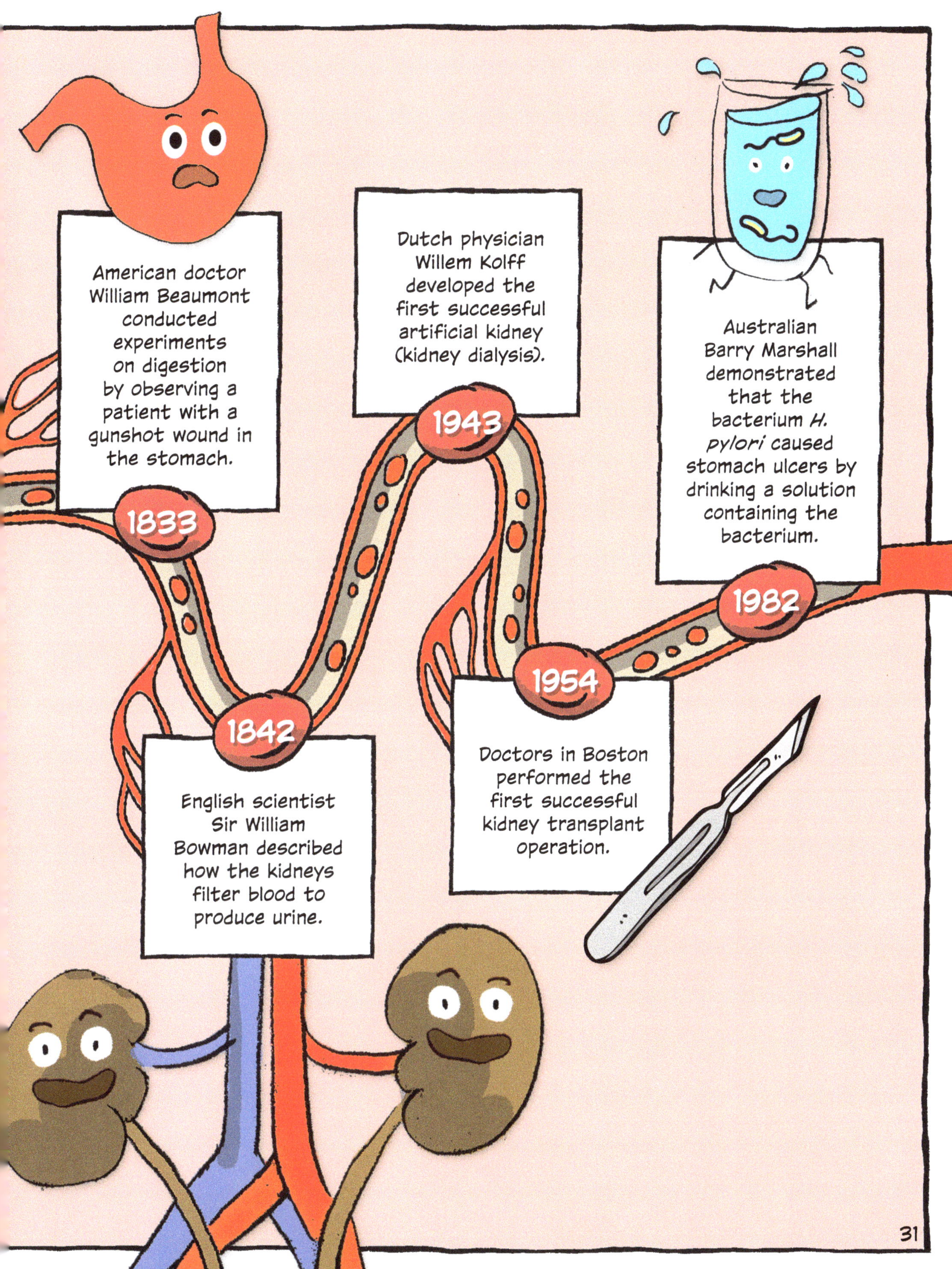
1833
American doctor William Beaumont conducted experiments on digestion by observing a patient with a gunshot wound in the stomach.
1842
English scientist Sir William Bowman described how the kidneys filter blood to produce urine.
1943
Dutch physician Willem Kolff developed the first successful artificial kidney (kidney dialysis).
1954
Doctors in Boston performed the first successful kidney transplant operation.
1982
Australian Barry Marshall demonstrated that the bacterium *H. pylori* caused stomach ulcers by drinking a solution containing the bacterium.

WHO'S WHO: WILLIAM BEAUMONT

My role in digestion was discovered in one of the strangest experiments in history! This is the story of Dr. William Beaumont!

Dr. Beaumont was a U.S. Army doctor on Mackinac Island in Michigan in 1822. His patient, Alexis St. Martin, had been wounded by an accidental shotgun blast.

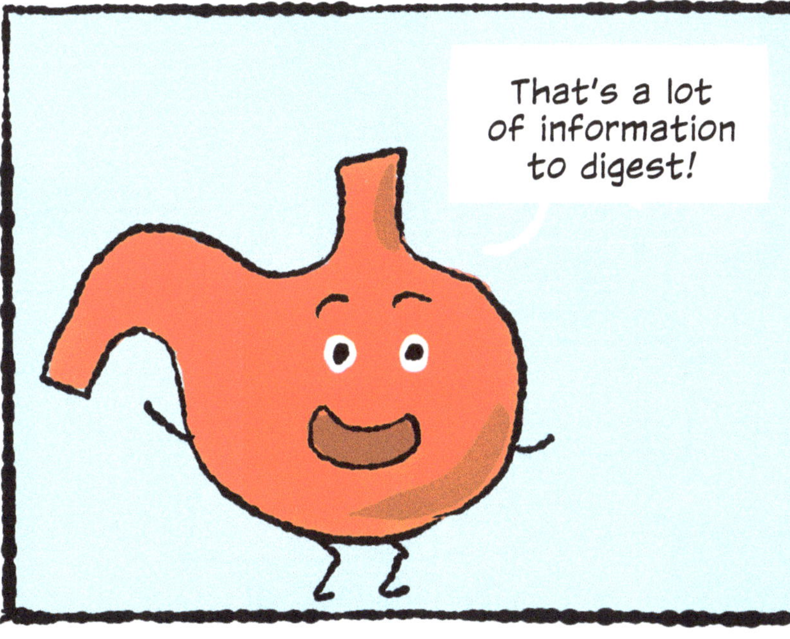

Fact File

Name: William Beaumont

Born: 1785 in Lebanon, Connecticut, USA

Occupation: Doctor

Claim to fame: Beaumont's book was the greatest single contribution ever made to our knowledge of how the stomach works.

ACTIVITY:
ONCE UPON A SWALLOW!

When Bertha Byal took a huge bite of a delicious dumpling, she had no idea that a large safety pin had fallen off the cook's apron and into her food. She rushed to the hospital with the pin stuck somewhere in her digestive system.

At the hospital, doctors probed, poked, and X-rayed the organs and structures that are part of her digestive system looking for the pin.

Bertha looked at the doctor's chart. Can you help her understand it? On a separate piece of paper, label the parts of the digestive system shown on the doctor's chart.

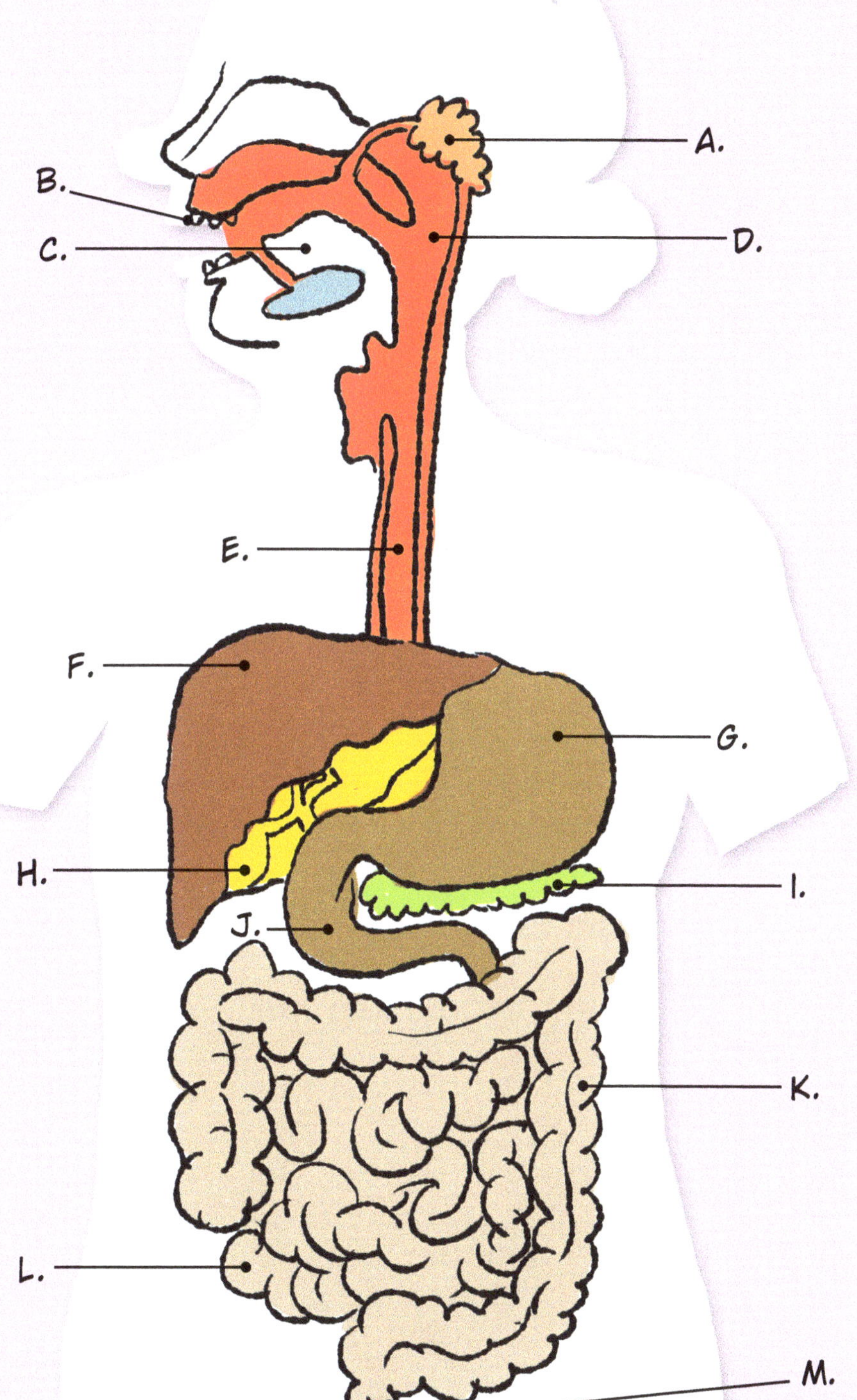

Pharynx
Teeth
Large intestine
Tongue
Liver
Salivary gland
Gallbladder
Stomach
Pancreas
Rectum
Esophagus
Duodenum
Small intestine

Did you label the parts correctly? Check the answer key on page 39 to find out!

CAN YOU BELIEVE IT?!

The muscles of the esophagus move food down to the stomach. This is why you can swallow even while **upside down!**

It takes about **7 seconds** for food to travel from your mouth to your stomach through the esophagus.

The length of an adult's **entire digestive system** is approximately 30 feet (9 meters) long.

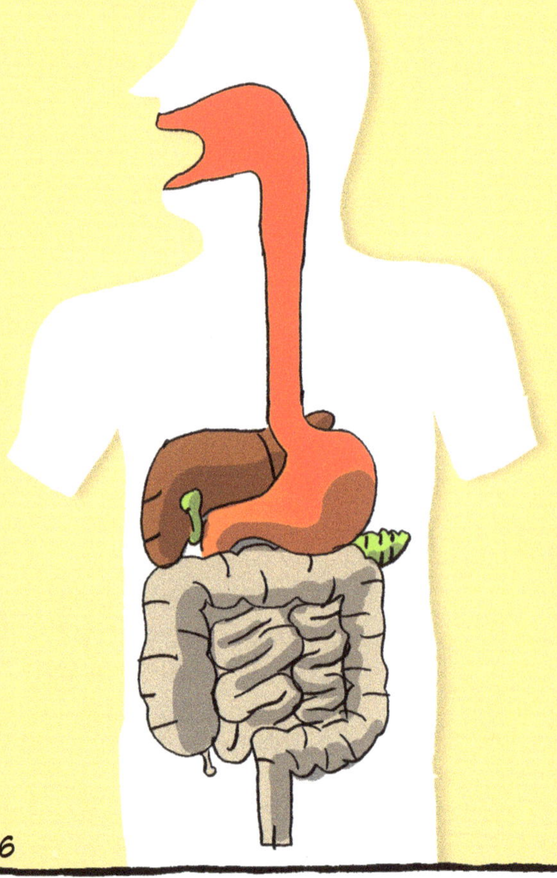

A normal or average person produces enough saliva to **fill two soda cans** every day—about 2 pints (950 ml).

Your digestive system has almost as many nerves as your brain. This may explain how you can have **a "gut feeling"!**

More than **500 different kinds** of bacteria live inside your digestive system. Most are harmless and many are actually good for you!

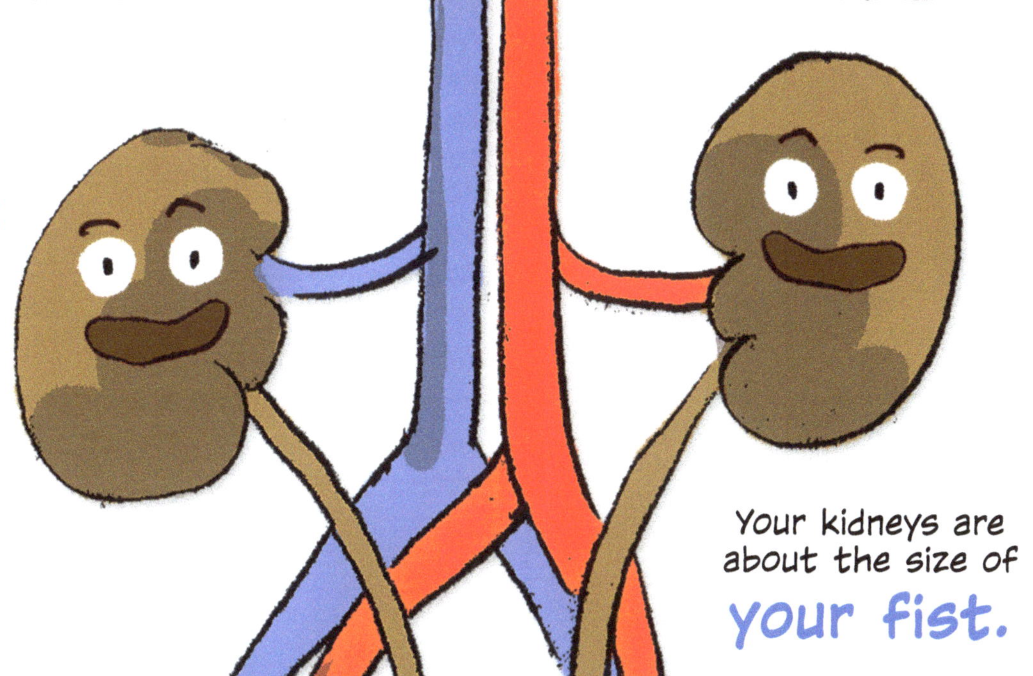

Your kidneys filter all of the blood in your body between **20 to 25** times per day.

Your right kidney is slightly **smaller** than the left kidney to make room for the liver.

Your kidneys are about the size of **your fist.**

Urine usually has a **yellowish color** due to a chemical called *urochrome.* This chemical is produced from the breakdown of worn-out red blood cells filtered out by the kidneys.

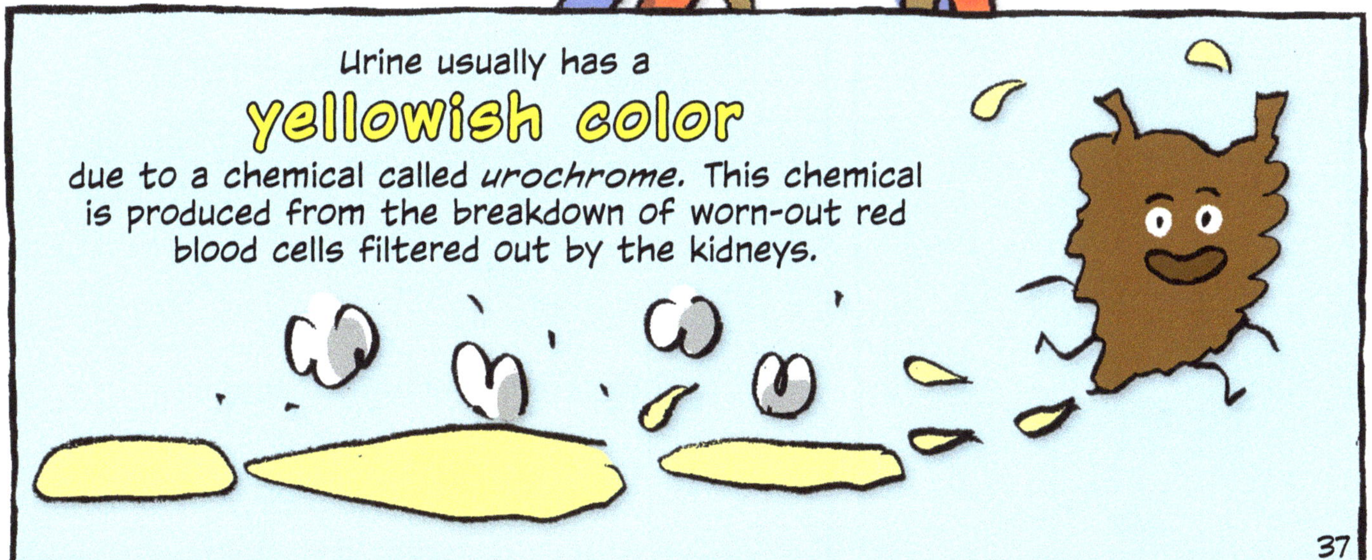

When your **stomach rumbles** it doesn't always mean you're hungry - that sound is caused by the muscles in your digestive system moving food, liquid, and gas around.

There are as many as 1,000 **small glands** in the mucous membrane of the mouth that aid in producing saliva.

If one of your kidneys stops working, the other one may grow to take up the slack. It may grow as much as **50 percent** bigger within two months!

Urine is heavier than water.

Most adults produce about **1.5 quarts** (1.4 liters) of urine daily.

WORDS TO KNOW

bacterium; bacteria a tiny single-celled organism; more than one bacterium.

bile a greenish-yellow liquid made by the liver and stored in the gallbladder.

bladder a hollow organ that stores urine.

blood vessel a hollow tube that carries blood and nutrients through the body.

cell the basic unit of all living things.

digestion the process where food is broken down and absorbed by the body.

digestive system the group of organs that breaks down and absorbs food inthe body.

esophagus a muscular tube connecting the mouth to the stomach.

gallbladder a small, saclike organ that stores digestive juices.

gastric juice digestive juice in the stomach that helps break down food molecules.

gland an organ that produces hormones or other substances.

kidney an organ that filters waste from the body to produce urine. The human body has two kidneys.

large intestine part of the digestive system that removes water and other materials from digested food.

liver an organ in the body that functions as a chemical factory and stores energy.

microorganism a tiny living thing.

molecule the smallest particle into which a substance can be divided and still have the chemical identity of the original substance.

nutrient a food substance that helps body growth.

organ two or more body tissues that work together to do a certain job.

pancreas an organ near the stomach that produces digestive juices and hormones.

small intestine an organ that breaks down and absorbs food.

sphincter a ringlike muscle that surrounds an opening of the body, and can contract to close it.

ureter a tube that carries urine from a kidney to the bladder.

urethra the tube where urine leaves the body.

urinary system the group of organs that removes wastes from the blood.

urine a yellowish fluid produced by the kidneys.

villi tiny fingerlike projections that line the wall of the small intestine.

Activity answer key: A. salivary gland; B. teeth; C. tongue; D. pharynx or throat; E. esophagus; F. liver; G. stomach; H. gallbladder; I. pancreas; J. duodenum (small intestine); K. large intestine; L. small intestine; M. rectum

INDEX

www.ingramcontent.com/pod-product-compliance
Lightning Source LLC
LaVergne TN
LVHW060633110826
845147LV00014B/905
9780716650676